KNOW YOUR GOVERNMENT

The Tennessee Valley Authority

KNOW YOUR GOVERNMENT

The Tennessee Valley Authority

Alanson A. Van Fleet

CHELSEA HOUSE PUBLISHERS
New York • Philadelphia

KG7-003087

Library of Congress Cataloging-in-Publication Data

Van Fleet, Alanson A.
 The Tennessee Valley Authority.
 (Know your government)
 Bibliography: p. 89
 Includes index.
 1. Tennessee Valley Authority. 2. Electric utilities—Tennessee River Valley.
I. Title. II. Series: Know your government (New York, N.Y.)
HD9685.U7T385 1987   353.0082'3'09768   86-31738

ISBN 1–55546–123-9
     0-7910-0876-2 (pbk.)

Project Editor: Nancy Priff
Associate Editor: Linda Fridy
Art Director: Maureen McCafferty
Series Designer: Anita Noble
Chief Copy Editor: Melissa Padovani
Project Coordinator: Kathleen P. Luczak
Editorial Assistant: Constance B. Goodman
Production Manager: Brian A. Shulik

ABOUT THE COVER

Like the cover photos, the TVA's seal reflects the agency's diverse
responsibilities: helping farmers to work their land more profitably; protecting
the environment; providing reasonably priced electricity through hydroeletric,
coal-burning, and nuclear power plants; improving navigation on the Tennessee
River; and controlling floods.

CONTENTS

KNOW YOUR GOVERNMENT

The American Red Cross
The Bureau of Indian Affairs
The Centers for Disease Control
The Central Intelligence Agency
The Children, Youth, and
    Families Division
The Department of Agriculture
The Department of the Air Force
The Department of the Army
The Department of Commerce
The Department of Defense
The Department of Education
The Department of Energy
The Department of Health
    and Human Services
The Department of Housing
    and Urban Development
The Department of the Interior
The Department of Justice
The Department of Labor
The Department of the Navy
The Department of State
The Department of
    Transportation
The Department of the Treasury
The Drug Enforcement
    Administration
The Environmental
    Protection Agency
The Equal Opportunities
    Commission
The Federal Aviation
    Administration
The Federal Bureau of
    Investigation
The Federal Communications
    Commission
The Federal Election Commission

The Federal Railroad
    Administration
The Food and Drug
    Administration
The Food and Nutrition Division
The House of Representatives
The Immigration and
    Naturalization Service
The Internal Revenue Service
The Interstate Commerce
    Commission
The National Foundation on the
    Arts and Humanities
The National Park Service
The National Science Foundation
The Presidency
The Securities and
    Exchange Commission
The Selective Service System
The Senate
The Small Business
    Administration
The Smithsonian
The Supreme Court
The Tennessee Valley Authority
The U.S. Arms Control and
    Disarmament Agency
The U.S. Coast Guard
The U.S. Commission on
    Civil Rights
The U.S. Fish and Wildlife Service
The U.S. Information Agency
The U.S. Mint
The U.S. Nuclear Regulatory
    Commission
The U.S. Postal Service
The U.S. Secret Service
The Veterans Administration

INTRODUCTION

Government: Crises of Confidence

Arthur M. Schlesinger, jr.

From the start, Americans have regarded their government with a mixture of reliance and mistrust. The men who founded the republic did not doubt the indispensability of government. "If men were angels," observed the 51st Federalist Paper, "no government would be necessary." But men are not angels. Since human beings are subject to wicked as well as to noble impulses, government was deemed essential to assure freedom and order.

At the same time, the American revolutionaries knew that government could also become a source of injury and oppression. The men who gathered in Philadelphia in 1787 to write the Constitution therefore had two purposes in mind. They wanted to establish a strong central authority and to limit that central authority's capacity to abuse its power.

To prevent the abuse of power, the founding fathers wrote two basic principles into the new Constitution. The principle of federalism divided power between the state governments and the central authority. The principle of the separation of powers subdivided the central authority itself into three branches—the executive, the legislative, and the judiciary—so that "each may be a check on the other." The *Know Your Government* series focuses on the major executive departments and agencies in these branches of the federal government.

The Constitution did not plan the executive branch in any detail. After vesting the executive power in the president, it assumed the existence of "executive departments" without specifying what these departments should be. Congress began defining their functions in 1789 by creating the Departments of State, Treasury, and War. The secretaries in charge of these departments made up President Washington's first cabinet. Congress also provided for a legal officer, and President Washington soon invited the attorney general, as he was called, to attend cabinet meetings. As need required, Congress created more executive departments.

Setting up the cabinet was only the first step in organizing the American state. With almost no guidance from the Constitution, President Washington, seconded by Alexander Hamilton, his brilliant secretary of the treasury, equipped the infant republic with a working administrative structure. The Federalists believed in both executive energy and executive accountability and set high standards for public appointments. The Jeffersonian opposition had less faith in strong government and preferred local government to the central authority. But when Jefferson himself became president in 1801, although he set out to change the direction of policy, he found no reason to alter the framework the Federalists had erected.

By 1801 there were about 3,000 federal civilian employees in a nation of a little more than 5 million people. Growth in territory and population steadily enlarged national responsibilities. Thirty years later, when Jackson was president, there were more than 11,000 government workers in a nation of 13 million.

The federal establishment was increasing at a faster rate than the population.

Jackson's presidency brought significant changes in the federal service. He believed that the executive branch contained too many officials who saw their jobs as "species of property" and as "a means of promoting individual interest." Against the idea of a permanent service based on life tenure, Jackson argued for the periodic redistribution of federal offices, contending that this was the democratic way and that official duties could be made "so plain and simple that men of intelligence may readily qualify themselves for their performance." He called this policy rotation-in-office. His opponents called it the spoils system.

In fact, partisan legend exaggerated the extent of Jackson's removals. More than 80 percent of federal officeholders retained their jobs. Jackson discharged no larger a proportion of government workers than Jefferson had done a generation earlier. But the rise in these years of mass political parties gave federal patronage new importance as a means of building the party and of rewarding activists. Jackson's successors were less restrained in the distribution of spoils. As the federal establishment grew—to nearly 40,000 by 1861—the politicization of the public service excited increasing concern.

After the Civil War the spoils system became a major political issue. High-minded men condemned it as the root of all political evil. The spoilsmen, said the British commentator James Bryce, "have distorted and depraved the mechanism of politics." Patronage, by giving jobs to unqualified, incompetent, and dishonest persons, lowered the standards of public service and nourished corrupt political machines. Office-seekers pursued presidents and cabinet secretaries without mercy. "Patronage," said Ulysses S. Grant after his presidency, "is the bane of the presidential office." "Every time I appoint someone to office," said another political leader, "I make a hundred enemies and one ingrate." George William Curtis, the president of the National Civil Service Reform League, summed up the indictment. He said,

The theory which perverts public trusts into party spoils, making public employment dependent upon personal favor and not on proved merit, necessarily ruins the self-respect of public employees, destroys the function of party in a republic, prostitutes elections into a desperate strife for personal profit, and degrades the national character by lowering the moral tone and standard of the country.

The object of civil service reform was to promote efficiency and honesty in the public service and to bring about the ethical regeneration of public life. Over bitter opposition from politicians, the reformers in 1883 passed the Pendleton Act, establishing a bipartisan Civil Service Commission, competitive examinations, and appointment on merit. The Pendleton Act also gave the president authority to extend by executive order the number of "classified" jobs—that is, jobs subject to the merit system. The act applied initially only to about 14,000 of the more than 100,000 federal positions. But by the end of the 19th century 40 percent of federal jobs had moved into the classified category.

Civil service reform was in part a response to the growing complexity of American life. As society grew more organized and problems more technical, official duties were no longer so plain and simple that any person of intelligence could perform them. In public service, as in other areas, the all-round man was yielding ground to the expert, the amateur to the professional. The excesses of the spoils system thus provoked the counter-ideal of scientific public administration, separate from politics and, as far as possible, insulated against it.

The cult of the expert, however, had its own excesses. The idea that administration could be divorced from policy was an illusion. And in the realm of policy, the expert, however much segregated from partisan politics, can never attain perfect objectivity. He remains the prisoner of his own set of values. It is these values rather than technical expertise that determine fundamental judgments of public policy. To turn over such judgments to experts, moreover, would be to abandon democracy itself; for in a democracy final decisions must be made by the people and their elected representatives. "The business of the expert," the British political scientist Harold Laski rightly said, "is to be on tap and not on top."

Politics, however, were deeply ingrained in American folkways. This meant intermittent tension between the presidential government, elected every four years by the people, and the permanent government, which saw presidents come and go while it went on forever. Sometimes the permanent government knew better than its political masters; sometimes it opposed or sabotaged valuable new initiatives. In the end a strong president with effective cabinet secretaries could make the permanent government responsive to presidential purpose, but it was often an exasperating struggle.

The struggle within the executive branch was less important, however, than the growing impatience with bureaucracy in society as a whole. The 20th century saw a considerable expansion of the federal establishment. The Great Depression and the New Deal led the national government to take on a variety of new responsibilities. The New Deal extended the federal regulatory apparatus. By 1940, in a nation of 130 million people, the number of federal workers for the first time passed the 1 million mark. The Second World War brought federal civilian employment to 3.8 million in 1945. With peace, the federal establishment declined to around 2 million by 1950. Then growth resumed, reaching 2.8 million by the 1980s.

The New Deal years saw rising criticism of "big government" and "bureaucracy." Businessmen resented federal regu-

11

lation. Conservatives worried about the impact of paternalistic government on individual self-reliance, on community responsibility, and on economic and personal freedom. The nation in effect renewed the old debate between Hamilton and Jefferson in the early republic, although with an ironic exchange of positions. For the Hamiltonian constituency, the "rich and well-born," once the advocate of affirmative government, now condemned government intervention, while the Jeffersonian constituency, the plain people, once the advocate of a weak central government and of states' rights, now favored government intervention.

In the 1980s, with the presidency of Ronald Reagan, the debate has burst out with unusual intensity. According to conservatives, government intervention abridges liberty, stifles enterprise, and is inefficient, wasteful, and arbitrary. It disturbs the harmony of the self-adjusting market and creates worse troubles than it solves. Get government off our backs, according to the popular cliché, and our problems will solve themselves. When government is necessary, let it be at the local level, close to the people. Above all, stop the inexorable growth of the federal government.

In fact, for all the talk about the "swollen" and "bloated" bureaucracy, the federal establishment has not been growing as inexorably as many Americans seem to believe. In 1949, it consisted of 2.1 million people. Thirty years later, while the country had grown by 70 million, the federal force had grown only by 750,000. Federal workers were a smaller percentage of the population in 1985 than they were in 1955—or in 1940. The federal establishment, in short, has not kept pace with population growth. Moreover, national defense and the postal service account for 60 percent of federal employment.

Why then the widespread idea about the remorseless growth of government? It is partly because in the 1960s the national government assumed new and intrusive functions:

affirmative action in civil rights, environmental protection, safety and health in the workplace, community organization, legal aid to the poor. Although this enlargement of the federal regulatory role was accompanied by marked growth in the size of government on all levels, the expansion has taken place primarily in state and local government. Whereas the federal force increased by only 27 percent in the 30 years after 1950, the state and local government force increased by an astonishing 212 percent.

Despite the statistics, the conviction flourishes in some minds that the national government is a steadily growing behemoth swallowing up the liberties of the people. The foes of Washington prefer local government, feeling it is closer to the people and therefore allegedly more responsive to popular needs. Obviously there is a great deal to be said for settling local questions locally. But local government is characteristically the government of the locally powerful. Historically, the way the locally powerless have won their human and constitutional rights has often been through appeal to the national government. The national government has vindicated racial justice against local bigotry, defended the Bill of Rights against local vigilantism, and protected natural resources against local greed. It has civilized industry and secured the rights of labor organizations. Had the states' rights creed prevailed, there would perhaps still be slavery in the United States.

The national authority, far from diminishing the individual, has given most Americans more personal dignity and liberty than ever before. The individual freedoms destroyed by the increase in national authority have been in the main the freedom to deny black Americans their rights as citizens; the freedom to put small children to work in mills and immigrants in sweatshops; the freedom to pay starvation wages, require barbarous working hours, and permit squalid working conditions; the freedom to deceive in the sale of goods and securities; the

13

freedom to pollute the environment—all freedoms that, one supposes, a civilized nation can readily do without.

"Statements are made," said President John F. Kennedy in 1963, "labelling the Federal Government an outsider, an intruder, an adversary. . . . The United States Government is not a stranger or not an enemy. It is the people of fifty states joining in a national effort. . . . Only a great national effort by a great people working together can explore the mysteries of space, harvest the products at the bottom of the ocean, and mobilize the human, natural, and material resources of our lands."

So an old debate continues. However, Americans are of two minds. When pollsters ask large, spacious questions—Do you think government has become too involved in your lives? Do you think government should stop regulating business?—a sizable majority opposes big government. But when asked specific questions about the practical work of government—Do you favor social security? unemployment compensation? Medicare? health and safety standards in factories? environmental protection? government guarantee of jobs for everyone seeking employment? price and wage controls when inflation threatens?—a sizable majority approves of intervention.

In general, Americans do not want less government. What they want is more efficient government. They want government to do a better job. For a time in the 1970s, with Vietnam and Watergate, Americans lost confidence in the national government. In 1964, more than three-quarters of those polled had thought the national government could be trusted to do right most of the time. By 1980 only one-quarter was prepared to offer such trust. But by 1984 trust in the federal government to manage national affairs had climbed back to 45 percent.

Bureaucracy is a term of abuse. But it is impossible to run any large organization, whether public or private, without a bureaucracy's division of labor and hierarchy of authority. And we live in a world of large organizations. Without bureaucracy modern society would collapse. The problem is not to abolish bureaucracy, but to make it flexible, efficient, and capable of innovation.

Two hundred years after the drafting of the Constitution, Americans still regard government with a mixture of reliance and mistrust—a good combination. Mistrust is the best way to keep government reliable. Informed criticism is the means of correcting governmental inefficiency, incompetence, and arbitrariness; that is, of best enabling government to play its essential role. For without government, we cannot attain the goals of the founding fathers. Without an understanding of government, we cannot have the informed criticism that makes government do the job right. It is the duty of every American citizen to *Know Your Government*—which is what this series is all about.

The TVA created reservoirs like the one above, as well as dams and other projects that changed the Tennessee Valley.

ONE

An Agency in a Land of Contrasts

The Tennessee Valley Authority (TVA)—a multifaceted agency—reflects the nature of the land it was named for. A land of great variety and contrasts, rugged mountains and green forests cover its eastern part, while open fields, rolling hills, flat farmland, and timberland lie in the west. Coal mines and aluminum plants, cotton fields and research centers, backwoods mountaineers and city slickers—these contrasting elements make up the Tennessee Valley. It includes parts of seven states: Alabama, Georgia, Kentucky, Mississippi, North Carolina, Virginia, and of course, Tennessee.

The Tennessee Valley extends for 650 miles (1,040 kilometers) along the Tennessee River and its tributaries, which together form America's fifth-largest river system. Along its crescent-shaped path, the Tennessee River rolls through some of America's most beautiful mountains and forests and through some of the South's most prominent cities. But it also flows through many polluted, poverty-stricken areas. This economic

The Tennessee Valley Region

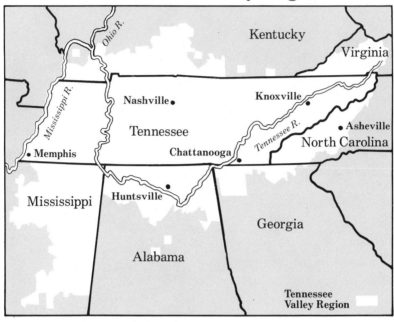

and ecologic diversity presented a challenge and an opportunity to proponents of regional planning in the 1930s. Seizing the moment, Franklin D. Roosevelt's New Deal administration created the TVA. It intended this agency to serve as the model for future regional development across the country.

The TVA was designed to improve regional conditions—by enabling river navigation, controlling frequent flooding, and producing electricity—and to serve the nation as a testing ground for new ideas. From the beginning, the TVA was an experiment in regional planning and in government. When President Roosevelt signed the TVA Act in 1933, he created a unique organizational design: a federally owned corporation that was part government and part business. In a message to Congress supporting the TVA, Roosevelt charged it with "the broadest duty of planning for the proper use, conservation, and development of the

18

natural resources of the Tennessee River [Valley] . . . for the general social and economic welfare of the nation." Indeed, the TVA has contributed to the region's—and the nation's—welfare.

For more than 50 years, this agency's responsibilities have been as varied and diverse as the region it serves. For example, in its early years, the TVA designed and built high-voltage lines to carry electricity to homes, schools, and factories throughout the Tennessee Valley. This system became the model for power grids throughout the country. Today, the TVA operates the country's largest electricity-producing system and maintains its role as an innovator in the utility industry. Electrical power from its plants travels along 17,000 miles (27,200 kilometers) of high-voltage lines—enough to stretch across the United States almost six times.

Its programs also help local communities create jobs, protect the environment, and maximize the region's natural resources. By its example, the TVA has shown people all over the country how to solve similar problems in their areas.

The TVA also developed techniques for measuring and reducing air pollution from coal-burning power plants, and many utility companies use these techniques today. The TVA's pioneering efforts have even extended to the research and development of new fertilizers and fertilizer production processes. Methods based on these processes today produce about three-quarters of all fertilizers in the world.

Although the TVA contributed to improvements across the nation, conflict and controversy often accompanied these contributions—and that, too, is part of the TVA's story.

In the early 1900s, Pinchot suggested that nature's resources be treated as a unit—an idea that the TVA later embraced.

TWO

The TVA's Historical Roots

During the nation's early years, many Americans believed that the land and its resources should be freely exploited. But, by the time Theodore Roosevelt became president in 1901, the costs of that belief were becoming clear. Roosevelt was keenly aware of those costs and believed that a nation that destroys its soil, water, and land destroys itself. As an example of his conviction, he helped promote the American Conservation Movement and established laws and government agencies to protect the country's land, water, minerals, forests, and other natural resources. He also convinced Congress to protect and preserve 150 million acres (60 million hectares) of government timberland throughout the country.

Roosevelt's chief forester, Gifford Pinchot, looked after these newly created national forests and helped establish a new way of viewing them. Until then, they had been treated as a separate, exploitable resource. Pinchot proposed that they be seen as part of a larger natural unity—that the water, land, for-

ests, farmland, and other natural resources were interdependent. Forests should not be thought of separately because they could not exist by themselves.

Pinchot urged government leaders to establish programs that recognized this natural unity and that managed the nation's resources according to this coordinating principle, rather than dividing them up and assigning them to different government agencies. Three decades later, Pinchot's ideas provided the framework for a national experiment in the integrated management of natural resources—the TVA.

Regional Conditions Before the TVA

When the TVA was created in 1933, the Tennessee Valley was one of the nation's most impoverished regions. Not everyone was poor, of course, but the average income in the region was less than half of the national average. The Great Depression had hit farmers and other rural residents hardest. The average yearly income for Valley farmers was $639 at a time when the national farm average was almost three times as high—$1,835. In one out of five Tennessee Valley counties, farmers earned $250 or less annually.

And the land was often as poor as the people. Centuries of outdated farming practices had depleted the soil's nutrients and encouraged erosion, which washed away the rich topsoil needed for good harvests. In fact, 85 percent of the region's cultivated farmland suffered from erosion. Gullies scarred 2 million acres (800,000 hectares) so deeply that some experts thought the land might never be revived. And many farmers didn't have the money or knowledge to correct the problems by using fertilizers and modern soil conservation practices.

During the depression, some Tennessee Valley families' annual incomes equaled only half the national average.

23

Erosion robbed farmland of valuable topsoil, and farmers lacked the technology to prevent the damage.

Poor timber cutting practices had stripped the region's forests in many places, and the Valley's mineral resources had also been crudely exploited. Clearly, the rural areas needed help.

The region's cities needed help as well. Some cities on the river, such as Chattanooga and Knoxville, faced the threat of flooding every spring. One observer described a particularly bad flood:

> There were steamboats sailing up Market Street in downtown Chattanooga. . . . Some of the two-story buildings were completely under water. . . . People and animals died, and there was disease [typhoid and malaria] because of the decaying vegetation and animals.

Wide fluctuations in the river's water level prohibited barge traffic during certain times of the year. And in some places, the river was never passable. For these reasons, the full length of

The Tennessee River overflowed its banks nearly every spring, flooding the streets of many riverfront towns.

the Tennessee River was virtually useless for navigation. As a result, the landlocked Valley region could not grow economically.

One place along the river where navigation was often impossible was near Muscle Shoals, Alabama. To encourage river traffic in this area, local officials had made three attempts to build canals—but all had failed. (One washed out and the other two didn't make enough of an improvement in the area.) After World War I, the Muscle Shoals area also suffered from a controversy over control of the Wilson Dam and two plants built there by the federal government to help produce nitrates, chemicals used to make munitions for the war.

Early attempts to make Muscle Shoals navigable failed.

Before World War I, America had imported almost all of its nitrate supplies from South America. But during the war, enemy attacks disrupted the shipping routes and cut off these supplies. In response, President Woodrow Wilson signed the National Defense Act of 1916, which included an order for the building of two nitrate plants in Muscle Shoals. To help supply these chemical plants with electricity, President Wilson ordered the building of a hydroelectric dam and other power plants.

Why did Wilson select Muscle Shoals as the site for this multimillion-dollar project? Because, at the time, experts thought it possessed the greatest potential for hydroelectricity east of the Rocky Mountains. In the Muscle Shoals area, the Tennessee River drops almost 85 feet (25.5 meters), and some estimates suggested that a dam there could produce as much hydroelectricity as a dam on the American side of Niagara Falls.

According to the original plan, the facilities were to produce nitrates to use for munitions during the war. But when World War I ended before the plants were completed, a controversy began to brew over control of the government facilities, including the plants, dams, and powerhouses. Some individuals wanted the government to keep the plants and use them to make nitrates for fertilizer to sell to farmers at a low price. But businessmen wanted to buy or lease the facilities and operate them for profit. One prominent businessman, Henry Ford, offered to buy the facilities and turn the area into a southern industrial mecca.

A bill supporting Ford's proposal passed the House of Representatives in March 1924. But when it reached the Senate, a Republican senator from Nebraska, George Norris, objected to the bill for two major reasons. First, he argued that Ford's offer of $5 million was too low because the facilities had cost the American public $130 million to build. Second, he objected to Ford's proposed use of the river. Like Gifford Pinchot and other conservationists, Norris saw the river as part of a natural unity. He wanted the Muscle Shoals facilities to be used as part of a

27

Congress, including this 1922 committee, debated during many sessions what to do with the Muscle Shoals facilities.

plan for the full development of the river system and for the benefit of the Valley residents. He replaced the proposed bill with one that held to these principles.

Between 1918 and 1933, Congress considered many bills regarding the federal facilities at Muscle Shoals, including several versions of Norris's bill. The House of Representatives and the Senate passed his first bill, but President Calvin Coolidge vetoed it. Shortly after he took office, President Herbert Hoover vetoed another of Norris's bills. Finally, Franklin D. Roosevelt—a president who favored the Pinchot concept—signed the seventh version of the bill into law.

The New Deal and the TVA

When Roosevelt took the presidential oath of office in March 1933, the most pressing issue his administration faced was the state of the nation's economy. America was in the depths of the

Great Depression. With the depression came a sense of urgency. Roosevelt recognized that conditions were ripe for bold government programs.

In his first 100 days in office, Roosevelt helped to create a number of far-reaching laws that formed the basis of the New Deal. The TVA Act was part of that legislative whirlwind. It incorporated the principle of natural unity proposed during Theodore Roosevelt's time. It also incorporated Franklin Roosevelt's view of an active government, in which government agencies would work with people to help overcome social and economic problems.

For many years, Norris tried to establish the TVA. The first dam it built was named for him.

Roosevelt signed the TVA Act in 1933 to help solve the ecological and economic problems of the Valley region.

Roosevelt saw the TVA as a practical way to unite these principles and believed that it could make dramatic improvements for the Tennessee Valley and its people. He hoped that if the TVA was successful, similar agencies would be created in other regions. And he believed the Tennessee Valley would be a good testing ground for these new ideas for three reasons. First, the region desperately needed help. Second, federal facilities already located in the region could provide a hub for the new agency's activities. And third, Congress had been planning to create a governmental agency to develop the region for several years.

Congress passed the bill despite stiff opposition. Private utilities opposed it because they feared a loss of electric sales when the TVA began to sell its own power. Some members of the fertilizer industry objected because they believed the federal government should not get involved in the fertilizer business.

Nevertheless, President Roosevelt signed the Tennessee Valley Authority Act into law on May 18, 1933. The act made the new agency responsible for flood control, navigation improvements, electric generation, fertilizer production, and agricultural and industrial development. It also charged the TVA with planning the advancement of the region's general social and economic well-being.

On the day the Tennessee Valley Authority Act established the TVA as a "federally-owned corporation," people danced in the streets of Muscle Shoals and celebrated with fireworks displays. They believed that better economic times lay ahead, as well as the end of years of controversy about their city's future.

TVA dam construction provided much-needed jobs, electricity, and inspiration during the depression and World War II.

THREE

The Building of the TVA

To establish and run this new agency, a group of talented engineers, planners, scientists, and technicians were brought together from all over the country. President Roosevelt selected three men to lead the agency. He appointed Arthur E. Morgan chairman of the TVA's Board of Directors. Morgan, an engineer and educator, had earned a reputation as a hardworking innovator. He assumed responsibility for programs involving river system development. David Lilienthal, a young electric utility expert, took charge of programs for producing and distributing electricity. Harcourt Morgan, who came to the TVA with a rich agricultural background and a vast knowledge of the region, assumed responsibility for the agency's agricultural and chemical development programs.

But soon, private disagreements arose among these board members and turned into public disputes. Chairman Morgan proposed to distribute TVA power through privately owned utilities, but Directors Lilienthal and Morgan strenuously opposed this.

A.E. Morgan, H. Morgan (no relation), and D. Lilienthal formed the first TVA Board of Directors.

They wanted to sell TVA electricity through consumer-owned electric cooperatives and municipal government-owned utilities, which would be more sensitive to residents' needs.

Chairman Morgan made speeches and wrote articles attacking his colleagues' integrity and motives. In response, Directors Lilienthal and Morgan passed a resolution condemning him for his behavior. Finally, when Chairman Morgan failed to provide evidence to support his claims against his fellow board members, President Roosevelt asked for his resignation.

Widespread awareness of the disagreements in the TVA forced Congress to investigate every aspect of the agency's operations. After two years, the congressional investigating committee dismissed Chairman Morgan's charges against his colleagues and reported favorably on the TVA.

Despite these conflicts during its first years, the TVA tackled three fundamental problems that faced the Tennessee Valley: floods, a lack of electricity in rural areas, and poor agricultural productivity.

Controlling Floods

The TVA inherited the Wilson Dam from the federal government and began construction on its first new dam less than six months after Roosevelt signed the TVA Act. Officials urgently wanted to get the dam underway to demonstrate that the government could improve people's lives during the depression.

This first dam was the Norris Dam, named for Senator Norris in recognition of his legislative efforts. It was located just north of Knoxville on the Clinch River, a Tennessee River tributary. One of the largest dams at the time, the Norris Dam was planned to help generate electricity in the Tennessee Valley. It was also designed to control flooding and minimize flood damage, much like other dams that were to be built by the TVA. To prepare for the flood-prone winter season, reservoir water levels could be lowered in the late summer and fall. Then the heavy rains of winter would refill the reservoirs and lie in storage until the drier months, when the water would be released without damage.

Within its first few years, the TVA earned a reputation for building dams in record time.

But unlike other TVA dams that were later built along the Tennessee River between Knoxville and Paducah, Kentucky, the Norris Dam was not built with navigational locks—gateways allowing river traffic to pass from one side of the dam to the other. (When the water level behind a dam is higher than the water level below it, a lock provides a stair step up or down into the next segment of the river. The lock opens on one side to allow boats to enter, and then water flows into—or drains out of—the lock to bring boats to water level on the other side of the dam.)

Work on the Norris Dam proceeded on a swift schedule. It was completed in 1936—in a record-breaking three years. A

Construction of the Norris Dam prevented flooding, but it also forced many people to leave their homes.

majestic 266 feet (79.8 meters) tall, with a 210-foot- (63-meter-) thick base, it was strong enough to hold back a reservoir with 775 miles (1,240 kilometers) of shoreline.

Although this dam's construction symbolized progress to Valley residents, this progress came at a dear price. To build the Norris Dam and fill the reservoir behind it, entire communities had to be abandoned. The construction forced about 14,000 people to leave their homes, and more than 5,000 graves had to be dug up and relocated on higher ground. A deep blanket of water was about to cover many farms, homes, churches, and graveyards. One resident commented bitterly that the TVA "scattered the living and raised the dead." Many others moved with a feeling of resignation.

The promise of progress and the heartbreak of relocation became even more familiar to area residents as the TVA's system of dams and reservoirs began to stretch across the Tennessee Valley. Three years after completion of the Norris Dam, the TVA had completed five dams and had five more under construction. Today, about 40 dams straddle the Tennessee River and its tributaries, controlling floods, generating inexpensive hydroelectricity, allowing river traffic to move freely, and providing opportunities for recreation and economic development.

Turning the Lights On

For those who lived along the Tennessee River, the TVA dams meant relief from the annual threat of flooding. But for the rest of the people throughout the Valley, they meant electricity.

During the 1930s, three-quarters of the Valley residents lived on farms or in small towns. But only three farms out of a hundred had electricity. Private utility companies found the cost of stringing power lines and providing electricity to sparsely populated areas so high that they could not charge enough to earn a profit. So they didn't provide electricity to these areas.

Before electricity reached the rural areas, residents did most farm labor and housework manually.

But people knew that electric saws, pumps, incubators, and milking machines would make traditionally grueling farm work easier and more productive. Pumps for running water and indoor plumbing, refrigerators, sewing machines, electric ranges, and washing machines could ease daily duties and change lifestyles forever. Electricity could provide a source of light and heat to combat the cold, dark winters. A man at a local church meeting best summed up the significance of electricity: "The greatest thing on earth is to have the love of God in your heart, and the next greatest thing is to have electricity in your house."

As described in the TVA Act, TVA-generated electricity was supposed to be used for TVA facilities, including the nitrate plants at Muscle Shoals. Then the surplus could be sold "at the lowest price feasible" to the region's people. To accomplish this, the TVA built transmission lines to carry electricity from its dams

After the TVA provided electricity to these areas, electric tools and appliances eased the daily struggle.

to municipal power systems and rural electric cooperatives that would serve Valley homes and businesses. The agency encouraged widespread use of electricity because it believed that the more electricity consumers used, the less it would cost to produce and deliver—in other words, the greater the total volume of electricity, the lower the cost per unit. And this was true for the TVA's first 40 years.

Solving Agricultural Problems

In 1933, most Tennessee Valley farmers were still using outdated farming practices and reaping very low agricultural yields. To correct these problems, the TVA began introducing the use of fertilizers and new farming practices through a program featuring demonstration farms. In exchange for free TVA fertilizers

Demonstration farms showed how new fertilizers and farming techniques could improve soil and crop production.

and technical advice, demonstration farmers agreed to adopt intensive, five-year farm management programs, to keep careful records, and to invite their neighbors in for tours.

Although farmers were skeptical at first, successful demonstration farms convinced many of them of the value of the TVA's programs. In some places, entire communities volunteered to serve as demonstration sites. Some counties eventually had 20 demonstration communities, with as many as 80 families participating in each one.

During the TVA's first decade, more than 15,000 demonstration farms produced yields that were three times higher than before. These dramatic successes spread from neighbor to neighbor, helping to usher in a new agricultural era in the Tennessee Valley.

In 1937, the TVA extended the availability of its experimental fertilizers outside the Tennessee Valley. Its "test demonstration" approach to agricultural improvement became a byword on farms from coast to coast.

Another important part of the TVA's early work involved soil erosion. To prevent and correct soil erosion damage, the TVA promoted three methods. First, it encouraged farmers to replace row crops on hillsides with trees or pasture grasses that would absorb rain and prevent the soil from running off. Second, it introduced terracing—step-like levels of turf or other ground cover on gently sloping land. Third, it recommended the use of lime and fertilizer to stimulate the growth of grasses and legumes that would hold the soil in place and provide feed for livestock.

Peaches and other produce grew larger and healthier with proper fertilization.

National and Regional Needs

The TVA wasn't even a decade old when World War II began. It entered the war years as a fledgling federal agency wedged in the hills and flatlands of the Tennessee Valley. It emerged after the war as the nation's largest supplier of electricity. But along with this transformation came many conflicts.

When the United States entered World War II, America's need for additional aluminum to build airplanes became critical. The Aluminum Corporation of America (ALCOA) had already established a plant in the Tennessee Valley, where most of America's aluminum was being produced. But the lack of large amounts of electricity limited further aluminum plant expansion— and therefore production.

By this time, the TVA had already demonstrated its ability to build dams—and build them quickly. So the federal government called on the agency to build additional dams to provide electricity for increased aluminum production, which would help build a stronger national defense. It also called on the TVA to supply large amounts of electricity for a "mystery plant" deep in the hills of Oak Ridge, Tennessee. This small town was the site of a key step in the famous "Manhattan Project," the top-secret project that was responsible for building America's first atomic bomb. Although the early research was done in New York—thus the project's name—the essential uranium isotope U-235 was purified here. This project's laboratories and plants required as much electricity as some entire towns in the Valley region.

Immediately after the United States declared war on Japan in 1941, President Roosevelt and the Congress approved construction of the Douglas Dam in east Tennessee. In less than 13 months, this dam was generating electricity for ALCOA and other consumers of TVA electricity. Fontana Dam in North Carolina's remote mountains was another dam built during the war. Workers labored around the clock in three shifts to complete the

During World War II, work on Fontana Dam continued 24 hours a day to meet the growing need for electrical power.

project as quickly as possible. During construction, a special public address system brought news, entertainment, and patriotic music to the workers.

Besides the Douglas and Fontana dams, the TVA started eight other dams during this period. It also constructed a coal-burning plant to provide a more constant source of electricity than the hydroelectric dams, which produced power that fluctuated with the amount of water flowing through them. By the late 1940s, about 140 electric cooperatives and municipal electric systems were distributing TVA power over 80,000 square miles (208,000 square kilometers) in seven states.

Wartime construction had made the TVA one of the country's largest power producers. Yet the demand for electricity

After the war, the TVA built coal-burning plants to supplement the hydroelectric ones.

continued to grow rapidly. Because few sites remained for major waterpower projects, the TVA began building very large coal-burning power plants in 1949 to meet the increasing demand. By 1955, the TVA's coal-burning plants were generating more electricity than its hydroelectric dams, and these plants were becoming the new symbol of progress.

As more cities and towns in the valley began to get TVA electricity, the TVA began to buy out the private systems. Although this expansion slowed by 1950, some privately-owned power companies remained concerned about the TVA's potential to take business away from them.

Trouble for the TVA

After the election of President Eisenhower in 1954, privately-owned utilities felt they had an ally in the White House. Eisenhower supported private enterprise and disliked government involvement. He appointed General Herbert D. Vogel chairman of the TVA's Board of Directors and sent him to the Valley with instructions to disband the agency.

At the same time, a group of private electric companies with boundaries on the TVA's service area forged a plan to sell their electricity within the TVA region. Edgar H. Dixon and Eugene Yates were key executives in this group that sought to challenge the TVA. Soon the private utilities and the TVA became involved in a bitter struggle that received national attention.

At about the time of this struggle, known as the Dixon-Yates controversy, the TVA was requesting funds from Congress to build a coal-burning plant near Memphis, Tennessee, to serve the city's growing electrical needs. Instead of supporting the TVA's request, the Eisenhower Administration supported the privately-owned utilities and proposed that they build a plant in Arkansas across the border from Memphis to serve the TVA region in and around the city. The electricity generated by this

Under presidential instructions, Vogel tried to disband the TVA in the 1950s.

plant would replace the TVA power sold to the Atomic Energy Commission's facilities near Paducah, Kentucky.

TVA Chairman Vogel supported this proposal, but many others—in Congress and in the Valley—opposed it. They argued that it would make part of the TVA region dependent on a power supply that had no obligation to the consumers. According to the TVA Act, the TVA was obligated to provide electricity "at the lowest feasible price," but it could not be sure of doing so under the proposed arrangement.

While the conflict raged between the private utilities and the TVA, the city of Memphis decided to build its own power plant. This reduced the need for an additional plant in that area, and the controversy subsided. (Memphis and its city-owned plant later rejoined the TVA power system.)

Moving Toward Independence

According to the original TVA Act, the TVA (unlike other utilities) could not sell bonds to finance power plant construction. Instead, it had to appeal to Congress for construction funds when they were needed. After the mid-1950s, Congress grew more reluctant to approve construction funds. It had to spend more money on defense because of the Cold War and had some difficulty justifying funds for coal-burning plants that served only one function, as opposed to multipurpose dams. Congress's reluctance made it difficult for the TVA to meet the region's growing need for electricity.

After several years of debate, Congress finally settled the issue in 1959 by amending the TVA Act. The new amendment allowed the TVA to sell bonds to finance the construction of power plants and also required the agency to repay with interest the money Congress had appropriated to finance TVA construction projects before 1959. This new financial independence prepared the TVA for yet another transformation.

Entering the Nuclear Age

By the time the TVA power system became self-financing, its coal-burning plants were supplying twice the amount of electricity as its hydroelectric dams. Some of the most modern and efficient equipment in the world was transforming coal into electricity at the TVA.

During the 1960s, more than two million homes and industries used TVA electricity. And the TVA's low rates encouraged households to use twice as much electricity as the national average. But problems arising from the burning of massive amounts of coal soon became evident. Coal mining endangered the lives of miners, and surface mining caused severe environmental damage. Also, large-scale coal burning polluted the air and threatened the natural resources that the TVA was supposed to protect.

Although strip mining gave the TVA coal to burn for electricity, it caused environmental damage.

But even as these problems were being recognized, the demand for electricity continued to grow. So the TVA took another giant step: It entered the nuclear age. In 1966, it began construction of its first nuclear plant—the Browns Ferry Nuclear Plant, in northern Alabama.

At that time, many experts believed that nuclear power was cheaper and cleaner to produce than coal power. Some nuclear power advocates claimed that it would revolutionize the industry, producing electricity so inexpensively that it would be "too cheap to meter"—not worth the cost of installing meters to see how much electricity people used. But as it turned out, nuclear power plant construction and operation were expensive and complicated, mainly because of safety and environmental considerations.

Plans for the Browns Ferry Nuclear Plant included three atomic reactors, which would make it the largest nuclear plant in the world when completed. Each reactor would be able to produce about the same amount of electricity as the largest TVA coal-burning plant. Soon the atom became the symbol of progress and technological success in the Tennessee Valley.

The TVA built its first nuclear plant at Browns Ferry.

The expense of building and operating nuclear plants caused the TVA to leave many of them unfinished.

The TVA's planning soon expanded to include additional nuclear plants to meet the region's expected needs. By 1975, six more nuclear plants were under construction or in the planning stages.

However, the TVA never built some of these plants. By the late 1970s, the cost of energy had increased dramatically, reversing the trend of growth in energy use. This reversal forced the TVA and electric power companies across the country to restudy their nuclear plant construction programs. Eventually, the TVA had to cancel three of its nuclear plants even though it had already spent billions of dollars on their construction. By 1986—the 20th anniversary of the TVA's nuclear program—only two nuclear plants had been completed and licensed to operate by the Nuclear Regulatory Commission. Two others were under construction.

All TVA power plants—whether hydroelectric, coal burning, or nuclear—generate electricity in a similar way. In all three methods, water serves as a basic component.

Hydroelectric dams produce electricity by allowing water to rush through large tunnels. The rushing water spins the giant blades of a turbine, much as a strong wind spins the blades on a pinwheel. The turbine then spins powerful magnets inside mas-

Hydroelectric, coal-burning, and nuclear plants all use huge turbine wheels to help generate electricity.

sive coils of copper wire. The magnets generate electricity by setting electrons inside the copper wire moving in the same direction at a high speed.

At a coal-burning plant, huge boilers burn coal to turn water to steam. The steam, under high pressure, turns turbine blades. After these blades begin to spin, the rest of the process is the same as that of a hydroelectric plant.

At a nuclear power plant, the concept is similar, but the technology is more complex. In these plants, enriched uranium fuels an atomic reaction, which gives off a tremendous amount of heat. This heat turns water into steam, which moves the turbine's blades. In nuclear plants water also plays another role: it keeps the nuclear reactor cool.

A Return to the TVA's Roots

From the beginning, the TVA was much more than a power company. It was an agency created to protect, develop, and wisely use the region's natural resources; to aid the region's social and economic advancement; and to respond to the people's needs.

However, in the 1950s and 1960s, the growing demand for electricity occupied most of the TVA's attention. Because of the tremendous growth of its power program, the TVA's regional programs received only a fraction of its total budget—and, some believed, its attention. Many people felt the agency was focusing too much attention on its power supply and not enough on its responsibilities for stewardship of natural resources, as prescribed in the TVA Act.

Problems with strip mining and air pollution from coal-burning plants soon presented a conflict between the TVA's commitments to natural resource protection and to low electric rates. Critics accused the TVA of not doing enough to protect the environment and of not taking the lead in dealing with environmental problems.

Air and water pollution presented a serious problem to the Valley until pollution control began in the late 1970s.

In the 1960s, the TVA responded by requiring coal suppliers to reclaim lands used for strip mines. This meant that the companies could not leave deep gouges in the earth where they had stripped away coal near the surface. Instead, they had to return it nearly to its original condition. This reclamation program was one of the first in the nation.

In 1978, after years of debate over air-pollution control methods and costs, citizen groups brought a lawsuit against the TVA. In an out-of-court settlement, the agency agreed to reduce the pollution from its coal plants by half. The resulting pollution control program—the largest of any utility in the country—took five years to complete, reduced pollutants by more than a million tons per year, and became a model for other power systems.

Although these environmental gains helped the region and its people, they also increased the cost of producing power. Today, the TVA's annual air-pollution control efforts cost about as much as its total power production did in the early 1970s.

This land in Bledsoe County, Tennessee, had been strip mined, but the planting of new trees helped to reclaim it.

In the late 1970s, the TVA began meeting regularly with environmental groups. It also started getting proposals from them and from other Valley interests for TVA actions and policies that would protect the region's air, water, and land. At the same time, the agency began to emphasize an open administration policy. It opened its Board of Directors meetings to the public and held public meetings throughout the Valley to inform people and involve them in its decision-making process.

The public can attend Board of Directors meetings to express opinions about TVA programs.

For example, one dilemma facing the TVA concerned the fate of the nuclear plants it had under construction. They were no longer needed and too expensive to build, but residents of the areas near these plants wanted construction to continue because this provided thousands of jobs. But after a series of public meetings, many realized that continuing construction could waste billions of dollars. Eventually, the public and the board jointly decided to halt the construction of three nuclear plants.

Although most TVA programs of the 1970s represented a return to the agency's roots, there were some exceptions. For example, when the TVA had begun its electrification programs in the 1930s, it had encouraged people to use more electricity, not less. The agency had reasoned that increased use of electricity would keep costs down through more efficient use of power plants and transmission lines. But in the 1970s, increased construction costs and high interest rates pushed the cost of building new plants skyward. In fact, it became so expensive that it drove the average cost of electricity up, not down.

So, the TVA began one of the country's most ambitious energy conservation programs. Since then, the TVA has provided energy efficiency inspections to about one million Valley homes and recommended ways for them to save electricity. It has also financed energy conservation measures with low-interest or interest-free loans.

Thus, the agency that used to promote widespread use of electricity today encourages energy conservation. The agency that once generated electricity solely by hydroelectric dams now depends on coal-fired plants and nuclear plants as well. And the agency that was founded on the principle of natural unity struggles to balance its roles as a utility and as a protector of natural resources.

From the TVA's corporate headquarters in Knoxville, the Board of Directors oversees the agency's activities.

FOUR

A Part-Business, Part-Government Agency

Unlike most other government agencies and departments, the TVA is a federal corporation. Its part-business, part-government status affects it in many ways. For instance, although the TVA's power programs are similar to those of private utility companies, the agency is wholly owned by the United States government. Like most private firms, the TVA's power programs must support themselves financially. But unlike other private enterprises, the TVA's other programs receive congressional funding. And like many businesses, the TVA has a Board of Directors. But in the TVA's case, the federal government selects it. In addition, the TVA reports on its programs and financial condition directly to the president and the Congress each year, and certain congressional committees see that the TVA carries out its programs properly.

The TVA's three-person Board of Directors heads the organization. The president of the United States appoints all board members, and the Senate must approve them before they can take office. Each member serves a nine-year term, but the terms are staggered so that a new member joins the board every three years as the most senior member leaves. To remove a board member before the end of his term, the president must ask him to resign or the Senate and House of Representatives must agree to remove him.

The board has four major responsibilities. First, it must establish and review the results of the TVA's general policies and programs. Second, it must approve the agency's annual budget and spending plan. Third, it must approve the appointment of key managers and maintain an organization for carrying out TVA policies and programs. And fourth, it must approve activities of major importance to the TVA or to the public, such as those involving the handling of acid rain and radioactive waste.

The TVA's general manager serves as its principal administrative officer. He is charged with a broad range of responsibilities, including making sure that the board's programs, policies, and decisions are carried out. The board appoints the general manager to office.

The general manager (standing) works with the TVA's board.

A number of corporate offices support the work of the general manager and Board of Directors. These include units that plan and budget, handle accounting, make economic forecasts, present public information, and maintain governmental relations. Other divisions handle such functions as employee relations, purchasing, and public safety.

The corporate headquarters also houses the general counsel and inspector general. The Office of the General Counsel advises the board and staff on legal matters, handles the agency's court cases and claims, and prepares and interprets documents affecting the TVA's legal responsibilities. The inspector general serves as an independent watchdog, reviewing the work of other TVA divisions and authorizing internal audits and investigations. Twice a year, he reports his findings to Congress.

The TVA's headquarters in Knoxville, Tennessee, contains all of the agency's corporate offices. Besides these offices, the TVA has four major program divisions. Two operate the TVA's power system: the Office of Power and the Office of Nuclear Power. Two run the non-power programs: the Office of Agricultural and Chemical Development and the Office of Natural Resources and Economic Development. Chattanooga, Tennessee, is the site of the main offices of the Office of Power and the Office of Nuclear Power. Muscle Shoals, Alabama, is the home of the Office of Agricultural and Chemical Development. And Knoxville is headquarters for the Office of Natural Resources and Economic Development.

The TVA's Major Offices

The Office of Power works to provide the region with a safe and reliable power supply at a reasonable cost to the region. It operates the TVA's hydroelectric dams and coal-burning and other non-nuclear generating plants, as well as the transmission lines that connect the generating plants to distributors and users of

The TVA Organization

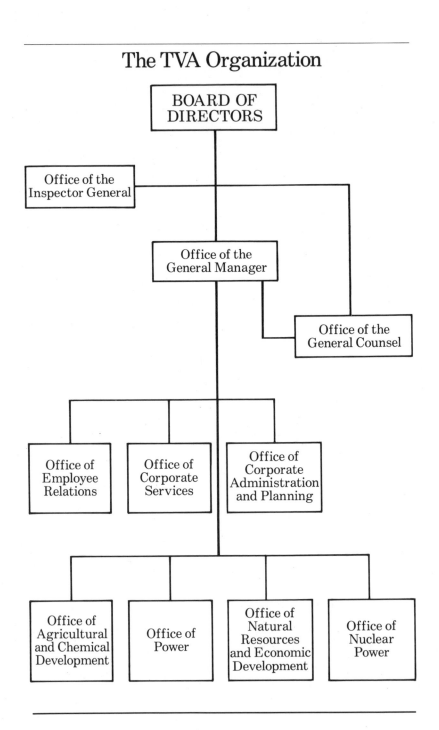

TVA electricity. It also manages the TVA's energy conservation program.

Additional tasks include predicting future electric demand, planning power supplies to meet that demand, and recommending electric rates for the board's approval. The Office of Power also tests new ideas in real-life situations. Among other projects, it tests and demonstrates various applications of solar energy, new coal-burning technologies, and even electric cars and vans.

Created in 1986, the Office of Nuclear Power consolidates in one office the design, construction, and operation of the TVA's nuclear power plants. (Previously, various TVA divisions performed these functions.) The office's chief responsibility is to operate the TVA's nuclear plants safely, efficiently, and according to Nuclear Regulatory Commission rules.

The Office of Agricultural and Chemical Development develops and tests new fertilizers and fertilizer technology. Its laboratories and plants at Muscle Shoals, Alabama, conduct all of this

One TVA office oversees fertilizer and other research.

research. In addition, the office works with private companies and universities around the world to introduce better fertilizers and more productive and economical farming practices.

The Office of Natural Resources and Economic Development promotes the social and economic welfare of the Tennessee Valley's people. It also preserves the quality of the region's natural resources—its air, water, land, forests, and wildlife. To accomplish these tasks, it cooperates with other government agencies to provide recreational opportunities and environmental education and to preserve cultural resources, such as archaeological sites. Within this office, the Environmental Quality Staff helps develop the TVA's environmental policies. It coordinates research and ensures that those policies comply with environmental laws and regulations.

Conflicts between the TVA's main offices have occurred often, chiefly because of the variety of the TVA's missions. For example, the Office of Power strives to provide electricity at the lowest possible price. To achieve this goal, it may want to take environmental shortcuts that undermine another office's duty to keep the environment clean. Or the environmental staff may

Another TVA office manages natural resources and economic development from Knoxville's old City Hall.

Recreational opportunities provided by one TVA office can conflict with the concerns of another office.

push for a land-use policy that would create problems for programs sponsored by the Office of Agricultural and Chemical Development. Or one TVA office may want to let water flow through the reservoir system quickly to maintain its quality, while another office prefers to let the water flow slowly so that reservoir levels remain high for recreation—meaning both fun *and* dollars for the local economy. (If the offices can't settle these conflicts by themselves, the TVA Board of Directors must evaluate both sides of the argument and make a final decision.) This "dynamic tension" is a vital part of the TVA, reflecting its unusually wide range of responsibilities.

TVA Funding

Funds from two different sources support the TVA's programs. The sale of electricity to customers and bonds to investors finances the power system. And congressional funds support the TVA's non-power programs each year.

The TVA does not sell its power directly to individuals, but to municipal distributors and electric cooperatives. The 160 distributors in the Tennessee Valley deliver electricity to about 2.8 million customers. Also, the TVA sells power directly to about 50 industries and government operations with very large power needs. The money from the sale of electricity pays for all of the power system's daily operating costs. But the TVA's system must also pay for capital costs—those required when a new power plant or transmission line has to be added, or when a large amount of money has to be raised for some other project. To meet these major capital expenses, the TVA sells bonds to the public or to the Federal Financing Bank.

As the TVA's power system has grown, so have its revenues and expenses. For example, in 1965, revenues from TVA's 160 distributors were about $271 million. In 1985, revenues from those sources exceeded that amount more than 10 times, and total revenues grew to about $4.5 billion. If the TVA were a private corporation, it would rank among the nation's 100 largest companies.

Tax money in the form of congressional funds supports the TVA's non-power programs. In the peak year of 1980, congressional funding topped $222 million. By 1986, that amount had declined to about $113 million.

The amount of tax money the TVA receives depends on the programs Congress and the president think are important for the region and the nation and the amount of public and political support the TVA has for its non-power programs.

Just as the TVA's funding reflects its status as a part-business, part-government agency, so do its responsibilities. It must reliably supply an essential product to consumers at a fair price while considering the long-term good of the region's resources, including its people. The TVA's overall structure as an organization also reflects this dual role: two offices are responsible for operating the nation's largest power system and two others are responsible for maintaining the TVA's economic, environmental, and agricultural programs. The TVA's unique structure is one of its greatest assets. And the diversity of the TVA's responsibilities, like the diversity of the region itself, is a source of its vitality.

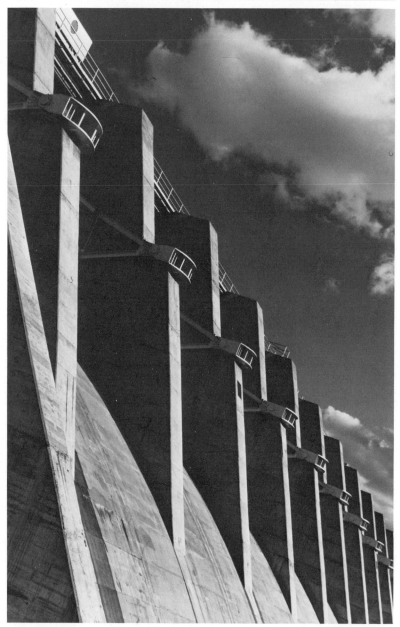

The TVA's hydroelectric plants, such as Douglas Dam, continue to produce electricity for the Valley.

FIVE

Today's TVA

Since its beginning, the TVA has been charged with many diverse responsibilities, and its role has remained wide-ranging. Today, the TVA continues to carry out its basic objectives, established in 1933. It still regulates flooding and improves navigation along the Tennessee River; develops new fertilizers and helps improve agriculture; aids in the conservation, development, and wise use of the Valley's resources; enhances the region's social and economic well-being; and provides electricity for the region's homes and businesses at the lowest cost. The TVA handles these responsibilities in various ways.

Developing the Tennessee River

The TVA's founders had a vision for the development of the Tennessee River. They saw a system of dams and reservoirs that would control flooding, allow year-round navigation, stimulate

In 1867, a record flood covered the town of Chattanooga (top). Today, the TVA's flood control system protects the city, as shown in the photo taken a century later (bottom).

economic development, and help make the region a better place to live. This broad vision still motivates the TVA's efforts.

The TVA's system of dams and reservoirs has prevented more than $3 billion in estimated flood damage since its construction. For example, in April and May of 1984 torrential rains fell in eastern Tennessee, creating the potential for the sixth-largest natural flood in the region's history. If this flood had occurred, the river would have crested almost 20 feet (6 meters) above flood level, inundating major areas of Chattanooga. But by storing water in reservoirs and releasing it slowly, the TVA prevented most of that flooding. In this situation alone, the TVA's reservoir system prevented about $700 million in estimated damages.

Floodplain management handles flood problems in another way. In this approach, the TVA works with local governments to help plan and zone their floodplains—the areas most likely to flood—to minimize damage to people and property. The simple object is to keep people and buildings out of areas that are likely to be flooded. The TVA's dams help "keep water away from people," but floodplain management helps "keep people away from water." Its programs have won national recognition and have been adopted in other parts of the country.

Besides controlling floods, the TVA continues to promote navigation on the Tennessee River and its tributaries. The improvement of locks in the TVA's main dams figures prominently in this program. If the TVA didn't maintain a year-round navigable channel, shippers of chemicals, coal, grain, and other materials would have to spend millions of extra dollars each year to move their goods through the region. The TVA estimates that

Locks adjust water levels, allowing ships to pass through.

since 1933, shippers have saved almost $2 billion by transporting their goods on the river. Since the TVA completed the channel in 1945, private industry has invested almost $5 billion dollars in waterfront plants, terminals, and distribution facilities. These waterfront industries have helped strengthen the region's economy.

The TVA's reservoir system serves another important function: recreation. Each year, millions of people swim, fish, ski, and boat on the reservoirs. Often called the "Great Lakes of the

Resorts have sprung up around the reservoirs created by dams, strengthening the recreation industry.

South," they have spawned a multimillion-dollar recreation industry along their shores.

Developing Agricultural Programs

The TVA's fertilizer laboratories at Muscle Shoals, Alabama, develop and produce new fertilizers and the technologies for making and using them. The laboratory's worldwide reputation draws hundreds, perhaps thousands, of international visitors to the center each year.

The agency's contributions in this field have helped shape the fertilizer industry and modern agriculture. Its National Fertilizer Development Center has developed more than 600 patents used in fertilizer manufacturing plants across the country. One of the center's best-known commercial products—ammonium nitrate—is used throughout the world.

Recent studies at the center continue to encourage further development in fertilizer technology. For example, phosphate is an important ingredient in many fertilizers, but mining has already depleted most sources of high-quality phosphate rock. Therefore, TVA researchers are testing ways to get more phosphate out of the lower-quality rock that is still available. These studies should ensure a supply of relatively inexpensive phosphate and save American farmers millions of dollars per year in fertilizer costs.

Current TVA research also seeks ways to improve nitrogen-based fertilizers. (Nitrogen is a naturally occurring element that plants need for growth.) Currently, much of the nitrogen in fertilizers never reaches crop roots because it evaporates into the air, washes away with water, or soaks too deeply into the soil. This loss wastes money and can damage the environment. Through chemical experiments and educational programs designed to change farming practices, the TVA is working to help farmers address this problem.

71

The TVA tests new fertilizers in the greenhouse before introducing them to farmers for use in the fields.

The agricultural part of the TVA's mission includes the development of programs for soil conservation and for the use of agricultural products and wastes as fuel sources.

An example of these efforts occurred when serious soil erosion developed in the western part of the region in the 1970s. The problem arose partly because farmers had substituted lucrative cash crops—mainly soybeans—for erosion-controlling cover crops. Also, some farmers had brought marginal land back into production. As a result, some fields in western Tennessee and northern Alabama and Mississippi were losing as much as 100 tons of topsoil per acre (36 tonnes per hectare) each year. So in 1979, the TVA began working with the United States Soil Conservation Service, regional land grant universities, and local farm organizations to demonstrate farming practices that would help curb soil erosion without curbing profits. One of these practices was "no-till" farming. Instead of the traditional method of plowing up the ground after harvest time, the no-till method encouraged farmers to let crop residues remain in the field, where they would help hold the soil in place until the next planting. Where these practices were adopted, erosion dropped significantly.

To increase the use of agricultural products and wastes for energy, one TVA project encourages farmers to convert corn-stalks, wheat straw, or forage crops, such as clover, into liquid fuels. The agency is also refining a process that turns wood into ethanol—a liquid fuel that can be mixed with gasoline. Several of these projects team the TVA with the United States Department of Energy.

No-till farming helps prevent erosion by letting crop remains stay in the field until it is plowed for the next planting.

Protecting Natural Resources

One of the TVA's founding principles is that nature and its resources should be treated as a unity. Consequently, the TVA functions as a land agency, a water agency, an energy agency, and an air quality agency. And government agencies and local communities cooperate in many of its programs.

The TVA supplies information about the environment and carries out a broad range of programs designed to protect the Tennessee Valley's natural resources. One such program involves water quality. Since 1936, the TVA's fact-finding surveys on water pollution and the subsequent reports it issues to each Valley state have helped provide the foundation for each state's water-pollution laws. Today, the TVA continues monitoring and reporting water conditions throughout the region.

Besides providing information, the agency tests new ideas and technologies to improve water quality. For example, the

Many TVA projects affect wildlife, such as these geese.

TVA is studying reservoir water quality. Normally, flowing water carries dissolved oxygen that supports fish and aquatic life. But when stored in large reservoirs for a long time, water can lose this oxygen. When the dam releases the oxygen-poor water to generate electricity, it affects water quality downstream. The situation can become particularly serious when a series of dams and reservoirs is involved. When the oxygen level declines too much, plants and animals in the river die. To correct this problem, the TVA is testing equipment that forces oxygen back into the water as it flows through the dam. These experiments have encouraged engineers and scientists to believe that this new equipment will eventually solve the water-quality problem.

Elsewhere in the Tennessee Valley, the TVA is working to determine how pollutants travel underground to reach groundwater supplies. About half of the water flowing in the Tennessee River system comes from groundwater, which is a valuable source of water for cities, industries, and farms. In rural areas,

TVA recreation areas are a natural habitat for some animals.

more than 90 percent of the water comes from wells fed by groundwater supplies. The TVA's experiments should provide valuable information about how to protect these supplies from pollution and how to clean them up if they do become polluted. The TVA is also working directly with a community in northeastern Tennessee to demonstrate how local citizens and groups can protect their own groundwater supplies. This project, involving local governments, businesses, and schools, makes residents aware of the importance of groundwater, tells how it can become polluted, and shows what can be done to prevent this.

All of these water-related projects reflect only one small portion of TVA's environmental concerns. Other projects—too numerous to mention—affect the region's land, soil, forests, wildlife, and air.

TVA scientists periodically test water quality.

The TVA attracts new industries and helps others to expand.

Enhancing Economic Development

Efforts to protect the Tennessee Valley's natural resources also help attract new industries to the region and help maintain the people's quality of life. In this way, the TVA's role in protecting natural resources goes hand-in-hand with its responsibility for promoting economic development.

The TVA also contributes to the region's economic advancement by maintaining and operating the main waterway, by providing electricity for factories, offices, farms, and homes, and by administering programs that help local and state agencies attract new industries. For example, it worked closely with the state of Tennessee to provide essential information for the planning of a multibillion-dollar factory built to produce the Saturn—a new General Motors car.

In addition, the TVA works with local electricity distributors to identify businesses in the Valley that could expand with help from TVA technical experts. In 1985, for instance, the agency helped more than 240 local firms expand, creating more than 10,000 new jobs. Since then, organizations in other parts of the country have adopted a similar approach.

The TVA's economic development strategy also involves targeting communities with the greatest need and helping them identify resources that can help them grow and prosper. The TVA targets certain areas of the region's economy for special improvement. Its current work with the forest industry exempli-

The lumber industry benefits from TVA training programs.

Home energy conservation inspections help keep costs low.

fies this approach. The region's forests present a great opportunity for economic development if they are managed properly and if the products are marketed adequately. So, in cooperation with the forest industry, the TVA offers training in modern forestry practices, advanced management techniques, and the marketing of Valley timber nationally and internationally.

Providing Electricity

Although the TVA's responsibilities are diverse, they often affect one another. This is especially true of the TVA's power system. Providing electricity is an important role. When most people think of the TVA, in fact, they think of an electric utility. About eight million people depend on TVA electricity, including thousands of businesses, factories, schools, churches, and hospitals.

79

Twenty-nine hydroelectric dams, 12 coal-fired steam generating plants, and 2 nuclear plants fuel this electric appetite.

The TVA's energy conservation programs, which are among the most ambitious in the nation, play an important role in its effort to provide electricity at the lowest possible price. The TVA estimates that its energy conservation programs have already helped reduce the demand on its electric system by the equivalent of one large coal-fired plant or one nuclear reactor. This has saved the power system and its consumers billions of dollars. Year after year, the TVA's rates remain among the lowest in the country.

But the TVA also concerns itself with the effects of electricity production on the region's environment and economy. A program that cleans polluting gases from its coal-burning plants exemplifies this concern. When coal burns, it produces sulfur dioxide and nitrogen oxides. These gases can harm the environment when released in large amounts and may cause acid rain,

Wet limestone scrubbers, which look like scaffolding, remove pollutants from gases before they enter the smokestacks.

which is known to damage crops and forests and to speed deterioration of buildings.

When the TVA became the nation's largest electric utility, it also became one of the country's largest consumers of coal and the single largest polluter of the nation's air. So in 1977, it spent more than a billion dollars on cleanup measures. These eventually reduced the TVA's air pollution by half, transforming the agency into a leader among electric utilities seeking to reduce air pollution.

As a power producer, the TVA affects the region's economy in two ways. It must provide an adequate supply of electricity to meet present and future needs, and it must price this electricity. The amount a business pays for electricity affects the amount it must charge for its goods or services. Therefore, the price of electricity affects how competitive a business can be and ultimately can influence its survival.

As part of its role in economic development, the TVA is experimenting with specially priced, "off-peak" power. During certain times of the day and certain times of the year, the demand for electricity dips. These times are called "off-peak." Some industries can rearrange work and production schedules to match peak effort with off-peak energy demands. By providing bargain rates during these times, the TVA's power system can help keep costs down for the region's large industrial consumers, helping them stay competitive. This arrangement also benefits the TVA—it can sell surplus power during off-peak times.

The TVA's programs and projects help it fulfill its mission to serve as a national laboratory testing new ideas and technologies. For example, in cooperation with several private electric utilities, the TVA is testing a boiler that burns coal more cleanly than a conventional one. If this boiler succeeds, utilities across the country will profit from the advance, and America will be able to take advantage of its vast coal reserves as an energy source for the future, while at the same time reducing air pollution.

The inscription above these generators, "Built for the people of the United States of America," reflects the TVA's mission.

SIX

Future Plans

Since its inception, the TVA has worked to help the nation and especially the people of the Tennessee Valley. Throughout America, TVA innovations are evident in energy production, in the management of natural resources, and in strategies for economic and regional development. And the Valley people themselves have benefited from reasonably priced electricity, flood control, navigational and environmental improvements, and economic development.

However, some students of the TVA argue that it has contributed relatively little—that other regions of the South have advanced just as much. Others argue that if the TVA had not done the things it has, state or local governments, or the private sector, would have stepped in. But the agency's accomplishments provide evidence that lives have been touched, the region improved—and the whole nation served.

The TVA has built the nation's largest electric power system, which serves a seven-state region with low-cost, reliable electricity. It operates a system of dams, locks, and reservoirs that controls flooding, provides for navigation, and stimulates development along one of the nation's largest rivers. It also serves as a national laboratory for innovation in the fields of agriculture, energy, and natural resources—helping to feed the world and provide electricity at home.

The era of massive TVA construction projects is over. In the near future, the TVA will not be building large, multipurpose dams or coal-burning plants. And once the nuclear plants under construction are finished, the TVA may not build any more of those, either.

Instead, the agency will concentrate on maintaining and operating its power system and making river improvements. It will also focus on its changing role in the region's economic development, especially regarding state and local projects. In addition, it will take a new direction with its agricultural programs, relying less on congressional funds and more on funding from other sources, such as the fertilizer industry.

From time to time, members of Congress introduce bills that would fundamentally alter the TVA—change its structure or eliminate some of its autonomy within the federal government. Some have suggested selling the TVA and allowing it to operate as a privately-owned utility. So far, the TVA's advocates have held the reformers at bay. The chances of Congress's adopting such proposals in the future depend on how well the TVA functions and the amount of support it receives from the public and its leaders.

A reservoir of support for the TVA exists among many people who remember the floods that once raged through the Valley, who remember what it was like before electricity reached the countryside, and who remember the outdated agricultural practices once common to the region. However, many other people remember the TVA as the agency that forced them out of their homes or flooded their farmland. Some remember the multibillion-dollar debt with which the TVA saddled the region's ratepayers to pay for its nuclear plants, some of which were not needed.

The TVA's future reputation will rest on its ability to navigate the changing environmental tides. But what challenges will

Construction of large power plants will decrease as the TVA focuses on lowering energy costs and on improving programs.

the future present? Many scientists and politicians claim that the availability of clean water will be a key issue in the years to come. Others believe that the nation's energy conservation efforts will be of primary importance. Still others argue that the management and disposal of hazardous wastes will be most urgent. And these are just some of the topics the TVA may tackle.

Throughout the world, the initials "TVA" stand for progress. For the TVA, this progress rests on a broad principle:

The TVA tests new methods of energy conservation, such as cars powered by electricity.

In the future, the agency will continue to manage resources—including buffalo and other wildlife—as an integrated unit.

All of a region's resources should be managed as part of nature's unity. According to this principle, the way an area develops and uses its energy resources affects the entire region's soil, water, air, forests, and wildlife. The TVA measures its progress by the sum of its accomplishments in all of these fields. But progress rarely comes without controversy. Gordon Clapp, a long-time general manager of TVA, observed that the TVA is controversial because it is consequential—it touches millions of lives. This is the responsibility that the TVA has carried in the past as well as the present and must continue to bear in the future.

GLOSSARY

Acid rain—Rainwater, polluted by coal burning, that can damage crops and speed deterioration of buildings.

Erosion—The washing away of topsoil by natural forces, such as rain and wind.

Floodplains—Areas most likely to flood.

Hydroelectric dam—A dam that generates electricity by the force of flowing water.

Lock—A channel that allows boats to pass through a dam or canal by adjusting water levels.

Nitrates—Chemicals used in fertilizers and ammunition.

No-till farming—The practice of allowing crop residue to remain in the field after a harvest to prevent erosion.

Reclamation—The process of returning land that has been strip mined to a natural state.

Strip mining—The process of mining near the earth's surface.

Terracing—Step-like levels of turf or other ground cover on gently sloping land.

SELECTED REFERENCES

Chandler, William. *The Myth of TVA: Conservation and Development in the Tennessee Valley 1933-1983*. Cambridge, Mass.: Ballinger Publishing Company, 1984.

Clapp, Gordon. *TVA: An Approach to the Development of a Region*. New York: Russell & Russell Publishers, 1971.

Hargrove, Erwin, and Conkin, Paul, eds. *TVA: Fifty Years of Grass-Roots Bureaucracy*. Urbana, Ill.: University of Illinois Press, 1983.

Lilienthal, David. *TVA: Democracy on the March*. Westport, Conn.: Greenwood Press, 1983.

Owen, Marguerite. *The Tennessee Valley Authority*. New York: Praeger, 1973.

Tennessee Valley Authority. *A History of the Tennessee Valley Authority*. Knoxville: Tennessee Valley Authority, 1983.

Tennessee Valley Authority. *1985 Annual Report to the President and Congress*. Knoxville: Tennessee Valley Authority, 1985.

ACKNOWLEDGMENTS

The author and publisher are grateful to these organizations for information and photographs: AP/Wide World Photos, Library of Congress, New York Public Library Picture Collection, Tennessee Valley Authority. Photo research: Alanson A. Van Fleet.

INDEX